CW00547909

S.U.M.M.I.T.

S.U.M.M.I.T.

Socially Upwardly Mobile Mountaineers in Training

or

THE NEW ENGLISH GENTLEMAN

or

THE SOCIAL SHERPA

or

GET BACK UNDER YOUR STONES SLOANES

being

The Official Social Climbers Handbook

by
DOUGLAS SUTHERLAND
Illustrated by Timothy Jaques

Secker & Warburg · London

First published in England 1986 by
Martin Secker & Warburg Ltd
54 Poland Street, London W1V 3DF

Copyright Text © 1986 by Douglas Sutherland
Copyright Drawings © 1986 by Tim Jaques

British Library Cataloguing in Publication Data

Sutherland, Douglas, *1919*–
S.U.M.M.I.T.: socially upwardly mobile
mountaineers in training.
1. Social mobility—Anecdotes, facetiae,
satire, etc.
I. Title
305.5'13'0207   HT609

ISBN 0-436-50602-5

Printed in Great Britain by
Richard Clay (The Chaucer Press) Ltd,
Bungay, Suffolk

Contents

Introduction

One of the most successful literary japes of all time was perpetrated, some years ago now, by Miss Nancy Mitford, when she sought to persuade the socially self-conscious that there were certain words in the English language by the wrong use of which the upper classes could instantly detect members of the non-upper classes, and brought into general use the shorthand version U and non-U which is now an integral part of the English vocabulary. It also had the effect of making the whole country class-conscious as never before.

Before you could say *bai-jove* or *gor-blimey* the whole country was split between upper and non-upper. In a trice matrons from Penge to Potter's Bar were hard at it trying to remember that they did not have mantlepieces but chimney-pieces in their neat semi-detached residences, each set in its own gnome-infested garden. Mrs Psmiths up and down the country were to be heard gloatingly asserting their social superiority over the Mrs Brown-hyphen-Browns, who had been heard, in an unguarded moment, to refer to a looking glass as a mirror:

> "Looking glass, looking glass on the wall
> Who is the fairest of us all . . ."

as the bard would have trilled in a more class-conscious age.

The unexpected thing about this explosion of absurdities was that it was taken with such deadly seriousness. Suddenly the whole of England seemed to be filled with people with a yearning to be recognized as upper class. As they stumbled over tripwire after tripwire, so cleverly contrived by Nancy, her coterie of friends rolled in the aisles with mirth.

"Kindly bring me some writing paper so that I can write a note to the milkman," was the sort of quote which had them choking over their dry martinis. Notepaper was, of course, one of the deadliest of non-U words.

The trouble with all this fleeting frivolity was that it refused to fleet. With the passing of the years the whole business of being U or non-U spread far beyond the bounds of mere vocabulary. The one-time trickle of social climbers roped together for mutual support on the icy slopes of the mountain has become an avalanche which, defying the laws of gravity, strives upwards to reach the highest peaks. In short, revolution is afoot.

When I first detected this trend way back in 1978 I thought it my duty to warn those eager to join the ranks of the upper classes just what was entailed. My series on the subject of English Gentlemen and their various relations was intended as an awful warning. Unfortunately it had quite the opposite effect. It sparked off a search for the Holy Grail of such proportions that the study of the English Gentleman in all his disguises became a minor industry. Books on the subject proliferated and the fever shows no signs of abating.

To climb socially is, all of a sudden, the "in" thing. The once proud boast of being "good middle class" has disappeared with the snows of yesteryear. Overnight there has sprung up a whole army of Social Sherpas desperately scrambling on the slippery slopes to find a ledge where they can rest awhile before continuing the upward struggle. False crests and treacherous crevasses abound – cruel traps far more devilish than any designed by Nancy Mitford.

Perhaps the most cruel of all the false crests was created with the invention of the Sloane Ranger. When that handbook appeared, young Sherpas, thinking themselves to be in sight of the Promised Land, rose to the bait like hungry trout to the mayfly. Suddenly the whole of suburbia was overrun by thousands of the socially self-conscious, perspiring in their Barbour jackets and green wellies, while their female equivalents, in Gucci headscarves and carrying their Louis Vuitton purses, caused traffic jams in the High Streets of Horsham, Highgate and Harrow-on-the-Hill. Insisting on doing their shopping in the local supermarket in their Range Rovers, they took care to display their Janet Reger underwear as they clambered out of the driving seat. Before long there were even a few of the species to be found nesting in Battersea or the other end of the Fulham Road, where the species had previously been quite unknown.

As they plunged deeper and deeper into the crevasse, once sober-suited City gents threw away their tightly rolled umbrellas, formerly the symbol of respectability, in favour of shooting sticks and took to sticking salmon flies in the bands of their bowler hats.

So deep has this crevasse proved that many despaired of ever climbing out of it and, resigned to their fate, settled down to form a sort of sub-culture. Latest reports indicate that they have even started to breed and that tiny Sloane Rangers have been seen scuttling about all over the place.

Others who have managed to avoid this not-so-tender trap have continued to search frantically for some toe- or finger-hold to enable them to claw an inch or two further up the mountain. Charlotte Bingham threw them a rope when she invented her Belgrave Square Set. There were also Wimps and Wallies, although I rather think they were all hell-bent downwards, set, like lemmings, on a course of self-destruction. Then there were, and for all I know still are, the Young Fogeys, a counter-revolutionary body to the Sloane Rangers, and, in an even more desperate bid for some sort of corporate identity, the Foodies, who appear to have resorted to gnawing their way upwards with their teeth.

Remorselessly the juggernaut moves on. Where once it was an unquestioned principle that it required at least three generations before being accepted among the top echelons of society, today it is claimed that it is something which can be achieved almost instantly, like Polaroid snapshots or microwave chips.

The oft-quoted dictum of Edmund Burke, "A

king can create a nobleman but he cannot make a gentleman'', suddenly seems as out-of-date as tomorrow's gossip columns. Just as any Harold, Ted or Maggie can create a dozen or so peers at the stroke of a pen, so it is reasonable to believe that, in these days of mechanization, computerization, insemination and commercialization, the field is open to anyone with the will and dedication to emerge from the pack and be acknowledged as belonging to the social class to which he so earnestly aspires.

But beware, Social Sherpas! Somewhere up there among the icy peaks, which, from below, seem to bask in eternal sunshine, there lurks a mysteriously remote race. They are the Abominal No-Men who jealously vet those who would aspire to join their exclusive circle and who are possessed of an almost uncanny ability to pierce the most carefully contrived disguises.

They are also armed with the very sharpest of shears with which, at the drop of an aitch, they can sever the mountaineer's rope and send the would-be *arriviste* hurtling on to the sharp rocks below, while the peaks around echo to their well-bred laughter.

It is to minimize the chance of such a disaster that I have produced this authoritative guidebook.

Douglas Sutherland

CHAPTER ONE

Sherpas International Inc.

It should not be thought that the first stirrings of the Social Revolution felt in England's green and pleasant land over a quarter of a century ago have remained an insular phenomenon. What was at first dismissed as a restlessness among the natives has since grown to earthquake proportions here and has not gone unremarked in other lands, not least in the United States of America. It is to them in particular that this chapter is addressed.

Sherpas of the World Unite

It is, perhaps, at first sight surprising to observe such a revolution among Americans, who have always taken pride in their classless society. All that was required if one was to sit at the top of the tree was to be dreadfully rich. There has long been a very small group of Very Rich And Important Americans who sought to distance themselves from their fellow colonists and who balanced on the head of a very small pin called *The Social Register*. This *Register*, comprising, as it did, some four hundred names, was so slim that it was hardly noticed when inserted in Macy's Department Store Christmas Catalog. It was widely disregarded by the peoples of this great democratic nation. It was quite unlike the enormously thick red volumes in which we British inscribe the annals of our blue-blooded families.

This is not, one would have thought, the climate which breeds revolution, but you can hardly buck the evidence, as they say over there. In America the Social Revolution is well and truly under way.

The truth of the matter is that the classless society has become thoroughly fed up with its own classlessness. Like all good rebellions, the Great American Social Revolution has been fuelled by a spate of inflammatory literature. One of the most recent and influential is a doctrinaire treatise entitled *Caste Marks – Style and Status in the U.S.A.*, by Professor Paul Fussell. The book swept through the class-starved American market like a prairie fire after a long drought.

Preppies and Yuppies

To assist in the further education of the revolutionaries, there came the *Preppy Handbook*, with the admirable aim of defining the Preppies' aspirations and, following this, in the current fashion of us British for classifying and labelling, they have come up with YUPPIES, which stands for Young Urban Professionals.

To be a Yuppy is definitely a term of social approval rather than opprobrium, more concerned as it is with improving social status than with making money. Surely the day cannot be far off

" I CAN'T HELP HAVING A CASTE MARK "

when one of the Ivy League Universities creates a
Chair in Yuppy, or, at least, appoints a Yuppy-in-
Residence.

The Fussell Scale

Professor Fussell makes some interesting observations on the number and variations of classes in
the new-look, socially aware, America. He claims
that the simple concept of a society divided into
upper, middle and lower classes, as is generally
accepted in less sophisticated counties, is woefully
inadequate. Sociologists, he says, have raised the
ante to five:

> Upper
> Upper middle
> Middle
> Lower middle
> Lower

Professor Fussell, a man who would have been
dear to the hearts of our nineteenth-century Victorians, who invented more and finer distinctions
between the classes than there are fleas on a hedge-
hog, favours a much more sophisticated definition. The Fussell Scale reads:

> Top out-of-sight
> Upper
> Upper middle
>
> Middle
> High proletarian
> Mid-proletarian
> Low proletarian

Destitute
Bottom out-of-sight

This assignment is in sharp contrast to that other increasingly socially-conscious State, the U.S.S.R. There, with truly Slavonic genius for simplification, they have only two classes:

Top out-of-sight
Bottom out-of-sight

Or, to go along with the new social shorthand, the Russians are divided into the T.O.O. and the B.O.O. This gives clear indication of an international awareness, however it may be expressed, that the attitude of the U-class, who have "Too" much, to the non-U class, is "Boo" – and this is certainly reason enough for revolution.

Target Practice

One of the most difficult tasks facing any revolutionary is to identify the target against which to revolt, and this applies equally to those striving, microscope in hand, to inch their way up the Fussell Scale as to the Ivans of the Russian tundra, who need a very powerful telescope indeed to identify theirs. When I wrote *The English Gentleman* some years ago it was not as difficult as it is today to identify the species known as Upper Class. After all anyone can identify a sitting duck.

That the English Gentleman took wing as a result of the barrage which ensued is not surprising. The result has been that those aspiring to move up the social ladder are faced with the difficulty of aiming at a moving target. Moreover, not only is the target twisting and diving in an effort to avoid being spotted, but conditions are changing all the time and the Social Sherpa has also to contend with the problem of climbing on moving snow.

Social climbing today is therefore a very tricky business indeed and may be said to be as difficult as trying to have sexual intercourse standing up in a canoe while shooting the rapids.

My object in addressing this chapter to Social Sherpas is that, in attempting to stabilize the image of the English Gentleman in a changing environment, I am trying to create for them an image towards which they, too, can strive.

For the sun has not set on the Upper Class English Gentleman – yet.

CHAPTER TWO

Official Warning to All Readers Now About to Embark on the Course of Instruction Which Follows

It has recently been brought to the notice of the author that that most highly esteemed work of reference, the *Oxford English Dictionary*, has sneaked on to the market a supplement to Volume IV, S–Z (published by the Oxford University Press at £90).

No objection is taken to the learned author, Dr Robert Burchfield, seeking to legitimize such words as:

se, an ancient Chinese musical instrument like a 25-stringed zither

or *Zyrian*, a tribe and its language from northern central Russia.

After all they have waited some thousand years for recognition and definition and, as the good Doctor points out, the policy has always been to "fend off overseas words until they have become firmly entrenched in British use".

Perhaps, in this new climate of intellectual liberalism, one can even go along with such American imports as "Whoopee Cushion", "a cushion which, when sat on, makes a sound like breaking wind", or "Yuppies", which readers of this book will have already discovered is transatlantic slang for "young, upwardly mobile people" or even "Y-fronts" which, we are authoritatively assured, is "a proprietary term for men's underwear, used especially to denote close-fitting briefs with Y-shaped seaming at the front". I, for one, am prepared to take his word for it.

Not so, however, when he comes to defining some of our most recently-forged words on the home front. Let us take one glaring example – "Sloane Ranger" is defined as, "of, or pertaining to, or characteristic of, a fashionable, but upper class and conventional young woman in London".

A more correct definition of this undeniably newly-established addition to our vocabulary might read: "of, or pertaining to, or characteristic of, a member of the middle classes anxious to be considered as fashionable as a member of the upper classes", which is quite a different cup of tea.

To be congealed in a permanent state of Sloane Rangerdom is now generally recognized as a cruel fate which one should not mock, but there are few among the current crop of social commentators who have much constructive advice to guide the footsteps of the serious social climber. Rather to the contrary. Only recently I read the advice of one such arbiter writing in one of our more socially conscious national newspapers. Pooh-poohing the regulation uniform of green wellies and Hermes headscarves, he went on to

FRIGHTENING THE HORSES

recommend suitable wear for a gentleman enjoying a relaxing weekend in the country: "A Jasper Conran herringbone tweed *blazer* (my italics) for a mere £320, with trousers thrown in for a further £175 and a silk spotted shirt (£220)." If that does not frighten the horses, I don't know what will.

Later, leafing through *The Tatler*, once the Parish Magazine of the Upper Crust, I came across an article by the Old Etonian (of course) restaurant critic in which he refers to the Head Waiter of a certain establishment as the *Maitre D*. With examples such as these thrust almost daily under the nose of the student of the art of social climbing, it does not put him or her in with much of a chance.

So be warned! Put not your faith in false prophets. Not even the supplement to the *Oxford English Dictionary*, Volume IV, S–Z (O.U.P. £90).

Read the only authorized definition of the English Gentleman in S.U.M.M.I.T. (Secker & Warburg £5.95).

BEWARE OF IMITATIONS.

CHAPTER THREE

The Nursery Slopes

Children are of the greatest importance to social Sherpas. Properly used, children are the entrée to many desirable places which would be closed to them otherwise. Without children, for example, the socially ambitious would not have the benefit of paying for an expensive education, for many valuable contacts are made with other upwardly mobile parents from the earliest kindergarten years onwards.

But, a word of warning! To be of maximum use on the social scene children have to be most carefully trained. It would be inappropriate in this work to discuss, other than in the most general terms, those mysterious forces of nature which are said to guide our destiny from the cradle to the grave, but it is difficult to have total belief in predestination. What cruel deity could decree that, with the cutting of the umbilical cords of two equally lusty babes, one should be destined in early adolescence to reach millionaire status as a drummer in a pop group, while his equally vociferous contemporary in the next cot should, after years of devoted service and exemplary conduct, rise to be a senior clerk in the Ministry of Pensions? That all sensible persons should envy the latter rather than the former just goes to emphasize how unfairly the cards of fate are dealt.

What is certain is that some careers require an early dedication of purpose not required by others. There must be few among us, for example, who dreamed away the halcyon days of youth against the magic hour when we could first take our place behind the shirt counter of the haberdashery store or be handed the broom of office to sweep up the clippings on the floor of the barber's shop.

Vocational Training

Just how early in life those born to vocations recognize the direction in which they are going to the extent of directing every waking moment to the furthering of their ambitions must vary. The embryo jockey who gallops round the nursery floor on his potty, the aspiring Thespian who declaims Little Bo Peep with actions from his crib, or the future politician who breaks all his toys and practises stabbing his teddy bear in the back with his baby-feeder must crop up from time to time.

Few children, by contrast, are born with such missionary zeal for social climbing. It cannot be expected of many, in their formative years, to evince uncontrolled excitement at the sight of a coronet-engraved envelope in Mummy's morning post or to smuggle *Burke's Peerage* back to school with them to study by torchlight under the bed-

" AND SEND US A CARD FROM WATFORD GAP SERVICES ! "

clothes after lights-out. It is clearly the role of the socially ambitious parent to guide the faltering early footsteps.

A Matter of Sex

If the foregoing observations appear to have been concerned more with little boys than little girls, this is natural enough. It is just that all little girls develop, at an early age, an ambition which goes far beyond the vocational, namely to marry a handsome prince and ride off into the sunset on the pommel of his saddle.

In this way, even if they do not live happily ever after, at least, at one bound, they can arrive at the top of the social tree and be a credit to their caring parents. There is little they can gain from the study of this book except in so far as it may help them, when eyeing any toad which may cross their paths, in assessing it for prince-potential.

The exception to this general rule is the little girl who is born so high up the social tree that she can aspire no higher. In many cases such girls are apt to develop an escapist syndrome. Handsome princes being the coin of their everyday life, many seek to satisfy their romantic ambitions in the hairy embrace of a muscular truck driver or a socially ambitious barrow boy. In their desperation to escape from the accident of their birth they strike out wildly at anything which comes their way, from hairdressers to night-club bouncers, people in television and even gossip columnists. This is a condition known in medical circles as Lady Chatterley's Complaint.

The Oedipus Role

The parental ambition to climb the social mountain via the nursery slopes is on the whole easier to achieve through daughters. Often it is just as simple a matter as joining the right pony club and putting horses under their offspring on every possible occasion. This will ensure that they make desirable contacts at a higher level, and, by and large, little girls take to this treatment more readily than little boys.

Even the Mrs Worthingtons who *will* put their daughters on the stage often emerge triumphant, while similar ambitions thrust on little boys can prove disastrous. Their attempts to guide them in what they may consider to be a socially acceptable direction frequently result in forcing their sons to emigrate or, even worse, to shave off half their hair and wear rings in their noses in protest.

Not a few children who do try to fulful their role as props for the social ambitions of their parents are apt to find too pushy a Mum a dreadful handicap. In a way it is almost as bad for a child to have too pushy a Mum as it is to find a Life Peer thrust upon it as a father.

Some guidance on how to avoid these traps in rearing the young will be found in the next chapter.

CHAPTER FOUR

Sherpas in Training

What's in a Name

There is a very great deal in a name. There is not much one can do about a family name which is inherited except to change it, and to change the family name is not really the done thing. The exception is in the case of actors or actresses whose ambition it is to project an image of themselves which looks good in bright lights. One can, for example, find no fault with Miss Diana Dors for changing her patronym to one more suitable to her role as the sex goddess of the silver screen. She was born Miss Fluck – not, as is sometimes alleged, Miss Clunt. Nor can one find much to quarrel with when a Mr Larushka Skikne adopted the pseudonym of Laurence Harvey, thus combining some of the glitter of his stage idol Laurence Olivier with the solid virtues of that up-market store Harvey Nicholls, which he happened to be passing at the moment of inspiration.

In the political world, too, it can be acceptable, as in the case of Mr Horeb-Elisha, who, by the simple manipulation of a hyphen, was to light a beacon to his memory as Mr Hore-Belisha when he became Minister of Transport. Less easy to follow is the process by which a war-time refugee from Czechoslovakia, Herr Hoch, after flirting with a number of rather more pretentious translations, eventually presented himself to the electorate as Captain Robert Maxwell, M.C.

However, these niceties need not concern the British-born with social aspirations. After all, having the good old family name of Wallop did not handicap the Mr Wallop who became first Earl of Portsmouth, and there are many other examples of the holders of unlikely names finding them no bar to social elevation; they would be most unwise to tamper with them now.

Permissible Variations on a Theme

The main exception to the stick-with-what-you-are-stuck-with rule is where you happen to have a family name which you share with so many of your fellow citizens as to merit a clearer identification, mainly for the convenience of others. Such names as Smith and Jones immediately spring to mind. There are, of course, many Smiths and Joneses who, through their own efforts, rise to become Generals, Judges and Professors and such like and are thus more readily identified when being looked up in a telephone directory. Some even become ennobled, which solves the problem. A certain William H. Smith, for example, found no difficulty in becoming Lord Hambleden and another Smith, a City Banker, also became a Peer, albeit an Irish one, as Lord Carrington.

It is not only acceptable but considerate for those with commonplace names to add some additional clue to correct identification by the adoption of another forename. Thus J. C. Smith could describe himself as J. Cunningham Smith or Bill Jones as W. Shrewsbury Jones and see to it that his name is correctly entered in the telephone directory and other works of reference as Jones, W. Shrewsbury. *Under no circumstances should the name be hyphenated.*

The hyphenating of names was a Victorian vulgarity much practised by the *nouveaux riches* of those days. It was sometimes carried to absurdity by stringing together three and even four family names in a desperate effort to distance themselves from the taint of self-made money, inherited wealth being a much more desirable commodity than the stuff one had made oneself.

It was a practice which really started out quite innocently, when a relative with a considerable fortune found him or herself without a direct heir bearing the same name and, desiring to perpetuate the dynasty, sought out a kinsman as the ultimate beneficiary on condition that the testator's name be adopted. This led to many *nouveaux* hyphenating their names like crazy in the hope that they would be mistaken for families of ancient fortune and high social standing.

The days when to make a great deal of money in one's own lifetime was an impregnable barrier to social advancement are now happily past, although traces of it still linger on, as is evident from a remark recently overheard in the Royal Enclosure at Ascot. A lady indulging in the age-old game of one-upmanship was heard to put down an acquaintance with the remark: "I would remind you, my dear, that my family have been *nouveaux riches* for a great deal longer than yours have."

On the whole, nowadays, to make a lot of money is quite the done thing and certainly something to be encouraged in one's children.

Today, although parents have only the most limited opportunity of passing on artificially distinctive patronyms to their progeny without making fools of themselves, the same is not true when it comes to choosing Christian names and this is an area where a few hints to Sherpa families might not come amiss. The rule is that simple, straightforward names are best. Most of the names of Christ's disciples are good bets with the exception of Judas which has been out of fashion now for nearly two thousand years. Any names which are common currency in the Royal family are acceptable and have been so since a Harold got one in the eye at the Battle of Hastings and a William took his place. Though acceptable, Harold has been well down the popularity list ever since.

The dangers of abbreviation should be watched. Oddly enough, it is the female of the species which suffers in this respect more than the male. Prince Charles ran a bit of a risk marrying a Diana, with its inevitable abbreviation to Di. Where Thomas, Richard and Henry can get away perfectly happily in top circles with Tom, Dick and Harry, somehow Florence, Gladys and Diana do not fare nearly so well as Flo, Glad and Di.

Incidentally, it is very hard on Prince Andrew (Andy) to have selected a bride with the eminently acceptable name of Sarah (Sally) to find her saddled with "Fergie", which is a term of

endearment usually reserved for retired nannies or
other family retainers of long standing. To give
girls nicknames, except under the most unusual
circumstances, is not a much accepted practice,
whereas it is the rule rather than the exception
that boys saddled at their prep schools with such
terms of endearment as "Blister", "Stinker" or
"Jug-Ears" should continue to bear the accolade
for the rest of their natural lives.

Another area in which great care should be exer-
cised when naming young Sherpas is to bear in
mind the dangers of carelessly chosen initials.
Victor should not have to suffer alongside Donald
as a second name, any more than Beryl would be
comfortable alongside Olivia. Winston Churchill
only just got away with it by slipping in a diplomatic S.

On the other hand, carefully chosen initials, or
rather the number and style of Christian names,
can confer considerable and memorable distinction
when they are reduced to initials on the school
list. To invoke a Saint is quite a good wheeze.
After all, where would a certain Mr Stevas of
Parliamentary and artistic fame have got without
the intervention of St John? The French "de" is
another effective device; it can always be attributed
without any fear of contradiction to an aristocratic
French grandmother, if not to an ancestor who
came over with William the Conqueror.

The number of Christian names is also important. It would be an uncaring parent who
confined the young hopeful to a single or even a
mere couple of initials. This is something which
can, of course, be taken too far, as was the case
with one fond father who gave his son all the

names of the Liverpool football team in honour of
their winning the Cup.

I can remember to this day the initials of the
boy who happened to be Head Boy at my own
Alma Mater in my first term. They were R. M.
St J. M., which, I thought at the time, was taking
things a bit far, particularly as he was also a Vis-
count, which was surely distinctive enough.

There is no doubt, however, that boys who have
three or even four initials look impressive on the
nominal role. In later years when Jones Minor
bumps into Smithers at a Royal Garden Party the
slow dawn of recognition is suddenly brought into
sharp focus, not so much by the recollection of an
ink-smudged face but by the name on the notice
board.

'Surely you are not . . . um . . . um . . . er?"

"Yes. Yes. Let me think now. You can't be er
. . . er . . . um?"

"By God! Dear old J.M.K.!"

"Well I'll be damned. It is R.W.L.P.!"

Slow fade as they embrace to background music
of "Forty Years On".

After, having had the commendable foresight
to give your young hopefuls a good start at the
font, comes the increasingly vexing question of
which school.

The Happiest Years of Your Life

It has long been held by those who consider themselves to have been disadvantaged in life that not
to have had a Public School education was the
greatest disadvantage of all.

By Public School, it should be explained for the
benefit of transatlantic readers, is meant private

or fee-paying schools, and that, generally speaking, the higher the fees the more exclusive and less public they are.

It is true to say that, from the point of view of any future advantage in life, to have been to a "good school" is no longer of such importance as it once was. No longer do the corridors of power echo to the cultured accents which were supposed to be the hallmark of the public schoolboy; no longer are the seats round the Cabinet table in Number Ten, Downing Street kept warm by successive generations from the same school. Nor is it necessary, to achieve high rank in the Army, the Church or the Civil Service, to have been to Eton or Harrow.

It should not be imagined, however, that a public school education is no longer of any importance. Indeed for a Sherpa to get his child into a public school is a *sine qua non* if he is to hold his head up at all in the company of his fellow Sherpas. It is really one of the main reasons for having children at all.

In former times the average English Gentleman did not, of course, send his son to a Public School for reasons of social advancement. He sent his boy to the same establishment as he himself had attended because he knew that he would be soundly whacked into shape and because it kept him out of the way in the pheasant-rearing season. He was not particularly interested in academic achievement. Indeed he was apt to become vaguely uneasy if his boy's name appeared too near the top of the class list. He would, however, be quite likely to vouchsafe a muttered, "Well done, m'boy" if he got his cricket colours.

All that has changed now. Parents, quite naturally anxious to get their money's worth, chatter on endlessly about the achievements, scholastic or otherwise, of their offspring. Mentioning the name of the particular establishment with every second breath, they make much of turning up on Parents' Day and gleefully recount what they said to the headmaster and what he said to them.

This is all fair game nowadays and, indeed, a necessary part of keeping up with one's fellow mountaineers, even if it does not cut a lot of ice with the *ancien régime*.

A Decent School

It is appropriate here to offer a brief survey of the public school scene as it is today, for this, like everything else, has changed greatly in recent years.

There was, for example, a time when Eton, closely followed by Harrow, was not only the most expensive but also the most desirable in terms of social advantage. Both schools boasted a tradition of sadistic savagery, sedulously fostered by former pupils who were prone to offset their own mediocrity by boasting of the number of prominent figures in public life who had either been their fags or whom they had taken the opportunity of beating.

The view generally held by the smelly socks brigade was that they were bastions of corruption, elitism and privilege, which bestowed on their alumni a grossly unfair advantage in life.

More impartial observers cannot but feel some

affection for the sort of school where an aristocratic pupil could complain rather diffidently that he was always beaten twice for the same offence – once for the offence itself and a second time for being a Lord; or for maintaining old-fashioned standards where to be caught jumping too low at leap-frog or smoking plain Virginian cigarettes behind the cricket pavilion was to face instant dismissal.

All that has changed. No longer are Eton and Harrow the most expensive of the expensive and no longer is it considered necessary to enter a boy at birth to be sure of gaining a place. In fact it never really was, but it remains one of the fictions dear to the hearts of Old Boys, like the asinine remark someone once made about the Battle of Waterloo being won on Eton's playing fields.

Nowadays there are several other establishments which vie with Eton and Harrow in bestowing social distinction on the parents of their pupils. There is Gordonstoun, for example, which was only founded just before the war but got off to a flying start by having Prince Philip as one of its first pupils. That he has since sent each of his sons there has done much to maintain its popularity with socially-conscious Mums, undeterred by the lurid reputation foisted upon it by the popular Press regarding the alleged toughness of its discipline. Presumably this misrepresentation owes its origin to the titillating thought of a Royal bottom being spanked, but it is quite without foundation. Gordonstoun is one of the wettest schools in this respect. Now that it has opened its doors to girls, many parents choose it as a soft option for their daughters, rather than expose them to the rigours of Roedean or Cheltenham Ladies' College.

Though discipline is now much more relaxed, it is only in the most eccentric and expensive establishments that the boys and girls call their teachers by their Christian names and class attendance is optional. In long-established, traditional schools such delights as nude bathing and the smoking of hash are still frowned upon.

How to be an Old Boy

I can remember an occasion at my own seat of learning when a well-meaning and distinguished visitor enquired kindly of one spotty youth what his ambition in life might be. The little beast replied, "To be an Old Boy, Sir."

In fact, it is not a bad ambition. The parent who has invested such a large sum of money on his child's education is entitled to the advantage of having a proper Old Boy for a son. By that I mean a youth who will address his elders with respect, be modest in his bearing, wash behind the ears and exhibit his old school tie on suitable occasions as an advertisement of the respectability of his upbringing. That it does not always work out that way is just one of the tragedies of life.

It would be invidious here to list those schools which are currently judged to be "in" or "out" by those members of the media who are always rabbiting on about such things. Even to name schools most likely to produce pin-through-the-nose pooftah-type Old Boys and those which retain the more traditional values might be taken amiss in some quarters. However, as some guidance should be given in this matter I have listed the more obvious advantages of a Public School education so respected by an earlier, more socially secure, generation.

1 You can rely on your boy getting his fair share of whackings.

2 A cold bath every morning (except Sundays) is compulsory.

3 In the winter term you have to defrost your face flannel every morning before use.

4 There are no locks on the doors of the bogs.

5 A substantial supper of cocoa and bread and marge is available last thing (6 p.m.).

6 There are no soppy girls.

If the dedicated parents will study the pages of the *Public Schools' Hand Book* and pick out a school which offers most of these facilities (none, I fear, nowadays score on all counts) then at least they will have done their best to give their offspring the sort of education to which a young gentleman of good social standing should be entitled.

Girls' Schools

With regard to schools for girls, any school which one of the Royals has attended will serve admirably, regardless of their academic standing or the facilities offered; also most "wet" boys' schools.

Jobs for the Boys

It should not be thought for a moment that the "advantages" of a Public School education extend to giving the end product any particular edge in the employment market. To have an acceptable old school tie hanging around the place should be reward enough for the upwardly mobile family.

On the other hand, the days when it was not really the done thing for members of the upper classes to engage in other than the most limited forms of employment, with the built-in understanding that none of them should be gainful, are long since past.

Acceptable Occupations

By the same token, jobs which were formerly acceptable, because of the low rewards they offered, like the Army or the Church, are still respectable ambitions for Sherpa offspring with sufficient brains.

Encouragingly, for the less talented whole new fields of employment have opened up which, until comparatively recently, would have spelt the total extinction of the social aspirations of the parents. Pre-eminent among these are the Metropolitan Police and London Transport.

It should be noted, however, that not any old Police Force will do, nor just any Regional Transport Authority. It will just not do for P.C. Plods with pretensions to an upper-class background to be found hammering the pavements in some back street in Manchester, any more than they should be discovered driving a bus in Newcastle-upon-Tyne. Even in the Metropolitan Police it is advisable to try for one of the more fashionable beats such as are to be found at Police Stations like West End Central in Mayfair, formerly an aristocratic playground where young sprigs of the nobility were wont to pinch policemen's helmets and knock off pedestrian traffic beacons on Boat Race night.

The Queen of the Line

Similar restrictions apply to jobs as bus drivers. Drivers only, please note. Bus conducting is not acceptable and nothing underground, not even the Tube train to Heathrow Airport.

Jobs as drivers on the better bus routes are so highly sought after that it is difficult to get behind the wheel of a Number Eleven, the Queen of the Line, which plies for trade along the King's Road in Chelsea, unless one happens to have been to Eton.

The number of Old Etonians operating on this route explains why the Number Elevens always arrive, at long intervals, in convoy. Old Etonians like to stick together. It is only a wonder that they do not all pull up in Sloane Square to join each other for their coffee break at the Royal Court Hotel . . .

Promotion Prospects

It would be wrong to think of such jobs as being dead ends. There have been shining examples of them leading to better things. For instance, when the talent scouts of Debrett's Peerage Ltd spotted a young Peer of the Realm working the Number Eleven route, which passes the end of their road, they had him demobilized overnight and he was promoted straight on to the Board of Directors.

As this work goes to Press there is news that an Earl and two Hons have just left the Metropolitan Police for lucrative new pastures. In the case of the Earl, the "pastures" were admittedly on his ancient family acres.

Something in the City

There is a job category vaguely described as "something in the City" which passes muster as cocktail-party conversation. It might mean anything from a tea boy in an insurance broker's office to one of those mysterious occupations which consist of selling or buying pieces of paper, preferably ten pound notes.

Despite the traditional resistance of the established upper classes to having anything to do with money (apart from marrying it), the changing face of the world in which we now live makes it quite acceptable, even for those with social ambitions, to indulge in "trade". Almost any merchandise will do providing you do not handle the stuff over the counter of a haberdashery shop or a greengrocer's store.

The Open Air Life

Top of the prestige table is any job connected with the countryside. This has connotations, as it always has had, with running the family broad acres between chasing foxes or keeping down the pheasant population. Thus landscape gardening, even when only applied to other people's window boxes, is very much an "in" thing, while things like interior decoration remain deeply suspect.

To embark on a career as a social climber from a standing start in the country is simply "not on". If you had the right country estate you would not be reading this guide. The shortest cut to ultimate acceptance by "the county", which still represents the most stubbornly-manned ramparts of the upper classes, is by becoming a land agent. Let it be noted that this does not mean an estate agent, which is quite a different kettle of fish. One of the few academic qualifications which can be useful to the social Sherpa is a degree in something like land economy, thus qualifying him to become an estate factor. This is a comparatively new opportunity for the social Sherpa which allows for living the life of a country squire while neatly getting over the difficulty of not having a sporting estate of one's own. In earlier times the only similar opportunity was to take a job as a gamekeeper and hope for the best.

A Limiting Factor

There are many jobs which need both ability and dedication and, perhaps for this very reason, have never rated highly among the careers favoured by the socially ambitious.

Basically, the professional man has his work cut out peering down the throats of the upper classes, praying for their salvation or tending to their bodily ailments or those of their animals, without leaving him time to worry about his own social advancement. On the other hand there can be no doubt that whole new fields of acceptable employment are now open to the socially ambitious.

Jobs for the Girls

The relaxation of the rules governing the sort of jobs open to the socially ambitious for their sons now applies equally to their daughters, only more so. The time, of course, has long since passed when the only hope for a girl of gentle birth who had hit a hurdle in the Marriage Stakes was to eke out an existence as a companion to some rich widowed relative, or seek premature refuge in a home for distressed gentlefolk. Considerable heiresses, however unfavoured by nature, never

" MY GOD – IT'S ANGELA ! "

experienced these difficulties. Theirs has always been the happier lot.

O Tempora, O Mores

All that has changed now. With heiresses desperately chasing barrow boys and model girls harbouring aspirations to marry Princes, the role of the female in our musical-chair society is in the melting pot and nowhere is this more evident than in Society with a capital S.

Among the lower classes women have always been hewers of wood and drawers of water, but the higher one went up the social tree the more unthinkable it became that ladies should take gainful employment. The hard-won right of women to become anything from a bookmaker's runner to a High Court judge or from a publican to the Prime Minister has opened the door for those with less well-defined ambitions.

In fact the pendulum has swung to the other extreme. There are now young ladies from the most respectable backgrounds queueing up for employment as anything from chalet maids in the Italian Alps to belly dancers in Djibouti, jobs which the average working-class girl would not touch with a barge pole.

The Marriage Factor

The traditional marriage equation among the upper classes, whereby young men of high social standing were urged by their impoverished parents to select a suitable marriage partner from among the daughters of wealthy self-made men who could afford to prop up the crumbling ancestral seat, is no longer valid.

Although there are not many ducal fathers today who are sufficiently rich to advise their eldest son not to marry a lady with big hands on the grounds that it would make his cock look small, the ritual of heiress-hunting among those "doing the Season" is now a virtually defunct tribal rite.

When our present Queen, quite early in her reign, abolished Court presentations, she not only threw a great number of young men, who were accustomed to living off the canapés and chicken legs which they had smuggled out of the debutante dances they had gate-crashed, on to the National Assistance but she made it impossible for young spinsters-in-waiting to sit at home with their petit-point. Now they have to get out into the front line where the action is.

It is no unusual thing today to find young ladies of high social standing doing things like playing the drums in a pop group or acting as a hat-check girl in a night club. These are now the sort of jobs in which they believe they are most likely to meet the largest number of eligible young men.

To Type or Not to Type

There was a time when to take a course in short-hand and typing was out of the question, or indeed in other skills which have now come to be considered to be all the go. To go in for modelling, for example, used to be regarded as only one step away from becoming a Soho stripper. To learn to type is now definitely "a good thing", if only as something to fall back on should one fail in the Marriage Stakes.

But beware of those advertisements which

appear so frequently in the columns of most Top People's papers which read: "Girl Friday wanted for busy, good-looking business executive who is going places fast. Opportunity for travel and to meet interesting people. Some typing skill desirable. Sense of humour essential." The only travel likely to come your way is a weekend in Paris and you are certainly going to need that sense of humour when the good-looking executive's wife walks into the hotel bedroom.

To Clothe or not to Clothe

Modelling is now an O.K. job, but if opportunity knocks for combining showing off clothes with showing off without clothes, make sure you only do the latter for the more blue-blooded photographers. There are any number of them to choose from. In fact it is jolly hard to become a top photographer nowadays without Royal connections. Just make sure the Press know all about it afterwards.

Skiing, Riding or Shooting?

As is the case with socially ambitious males, the open-air life offers many excellent opportunities. On the whole, however, the present craze among the Sloane Ranger type to take jobs as chalet maids in some of the more popular ski resorts is apt to be self-defeating. The only people a girl is likely to meet are other Sloane Ranger types stuck in the same social crevasse that sensible Sherpa girls are so anxious to avoid.

Messing around with horses somewhere in the Shires or sweeping-up in a Lodge in the Scottish Highlands during the grouse shooting season offers greater possibilities.

Job Satisfaction

It would, of course, be highly irresponsible to suggest that the only criterion for a young lady seeking a job should relate to its matrimonial possibilities – even in the loosest possible sense of the word matrimony.

In many cases job satisfaction is the major consideration. For example, in the nursing profession or even something as modest as looking after children in a nursery school, the job the Princess of Wales had before she was discovered by Prince Charles.

Other jobs for which young ladies of good pedigree are much in demand include publishing and public relations, with journalism and politics also well up the list.

The trouble with the first two is that pretty little things who start off with a light touch on the typewriter tend to get so carried away with job satisfaction that they rapidly develop into powerful ladies in their own right and devour their erstwhile male masters after the fashion of certain species of predatory spiders.

The trouble with the second two jobs, at least from the male point of view, is that the same thing happens, only with greater inevitability. That our most recent Royal bride, Sarah Ferguson, was in publishing and may have to give it up for love eventually is the exception which proves the rule.

CHAPTER FIVE

Clubs are Trumps

All social Sherpas should belong to a good club. Not so long ago it would not have been necessary to qualify the word "club" with the adjective "good", for it is not used in the sense of being the opposite of "bad". Perhaps "decent" would be a better description, were it not that it might be taken as a warning to avoid the indecent.

The truth is that it is the word "club" which now requires a more exact definition. The socially self-conscious Victorians used to describe them as "Gentlemen's Clubs" and it may be necessary to revive the term to describe those grim, soot-blackened fortresses which line Pall Mall and where, by tradition, senior civil servants from nearby Whitehall sleep off their post-prandial port before catching the early afternoon train back to their mock-Tudor mansions in the outer suburbs.

I suppose that those Pall Mall palaces still qualify as "good" clubs, but they are not a great deal of use as a ladder to the upper slopes of the social mountain. Basically, membership of those clubs is

a matter of horses for courses. The socially ambitious curate should spare no effort or expense to
get himself elected to the Athenaeum. He can
expect little chance of immediate success on account of the long waiting list of clerics anxious to
join the Bishops scrambling to have first whack at
the rice pudding.

The white-collar worker has a choice of several
"good" clubs which he might usefully join to
advance his career. The Travellers' Club, for instance, was originally founded for intrepid Victorians who could produce evidence that they had
travelled a hundred miles or more, measured in a
straight line from London. It is now almost the
exclusive preserve of officials from the Foreign
Office. Its main rival in recruiting members from
the echelons of office workers is the Reform,
where the mandarins of the Treasury are thick on
the ground. Both clubs traditionally have their
sprinkling of spies; Donald Maclean was a fellow
traveller at the Travellers' while Guy Burgess was
keeping watch at the Reform. There an extra large
glass of port was, until recently, known as a
"Burgess".

Even the Turf, which likes to hold itself aloof
in its Carlton House Terrace mansion, has been
known to house the odd spy – art expert Anthony
Blunt must rate as one of the oddest. "Just one of
the sods I have cut in the Turf," as a member was
heard to remark with a shrug when he heard that
one of his fellow members had been flushed out
and de-knighted.

Incidentally, it was at the Turf, which can
boast more Dukes to the square foot than any
other club in London, that the late Duke of

Marlborough made his now famous stand against over-familiarity. Enraged at being bid "Good Morning" by a young member with whom he was not acquainted, he rang angrily for the Club Secretary to make a bitter complaint.

"Good gracious," exclaimed the Secretary, who, in a club, must be all things to all men. "What did you do, Your Grace?"

"Well, I didn't want to seem rude," boomed the enraged Duke, "so I just turned me back and walked away."

By and large, however, the only clubs which can be regarded as giving the nod to social acceptability are those older and more elegant establishments in St James's Street. These originated as coffee houses in Regency days and were patronized by the more rakish elements of Society with nothing to do all day, and most of the night, but gossip and gamble. When they sought to isolate themselves from the hoi polloi by forming themselves into clubs they liked to cling to their old idle and dissolute image, so to be involved in any sort of gainful enterprise or to belong to a less than aristocratic stratum of society was to invite a veritable avalanche of black balls in the ballot box.

Only a dwindling number of clubs have managed to preserve this image of upper-class exclusivity in the cold commercialism of the post-war years during which so many other bastions of privilege have tumbled.

One of the first to go, after the last war, was the Bachelors', which drew its exclusive membership from young men of good family and fortune. Unfortunately, they could only remain members for as long as they enjoyed bachelor status. Under

" HE MUST HAVE WOKEN UP SUDDENLY AND CAUGHT SIGHT OF THE CHECK SIR "

post-war conditions the breed was so much in demand in the Marriage Stakes that they became so rare as to prove terminally destructive to their club.

On the demise of the Bachelors', the residual membership was offered accommodation at White's Club at the top of St James's Street, where the members still gather in the famous street-level bow window to enjoy the spectacle, in the words of Beau Brummel, of "the demned people getting wet outside". If White's was not to their taste the alternative was the St James's Club in Piccadilly, which enjoyed, by all accounts, a different kind of exclusivity. In its, ultimately vain, effort to survive the Club had offered honorary membership to members of the Diplomatic Corps accredited to the Court of St James and many foreign diplomats had availed themselves of the opportunity. At the same time it had the reputation of having more than its fair share of members whose sexual preferences tended to be for those of their own sex.

It is said that a young bachelor once asked the advice of a peppery baronet, who happened to be a member of the two clubs, which one he should try to join. He tactfully expressed a slight preference for the St James's, in which the baronet happened to be at the time.

"Nonsense," barked the Bart. "There are three types of member of this club. One lot are foreigners, another lot are buggers and the third lot are foreign buggers."

Alas for those with aspirations to join this select company, the St James's Club has joined the ever-lengthening list of casualties in the league of Gentlemen's Clubs. Rumour has it that the premises are now awash with foreign *au pair* girls learning English.

So what remains for the arriviste? The Service Clubs, like the Guards and Cavalry, or the actors'-lawyers'-and-pen-pushers' home from home, the Garrick, excellent although they are, insist on preserving their jealously-guarded exclusivity for their own tradesfolk.

The fate of one such, the Chelsea Arts, for many years the delightfully Bohemian refuge of artists and their friends, is still painfully fresh in the memory of the diehard clubman. Feeling the winds of financial adversity, the Committee decided to open the doors just a tiny crack ... Before you could say "Picasso", the whole place was overrun with Sloane Rangers, braying for ginger beer shandies and puking all over the garden. It may have moved the painters out fairly fast but at least it gave the Rangers somewhere they could call their own, which must rate as some sort of blessing.

Of the clubs which remain, it is probably only the three survivors in St James's Street to which the Sherpa might seek admission with a reasonable chance of success and which he might find are still regarded as a useful prop to his social aspirations.

There is the aforementioned White's, which, as its name suggests, is a highly racist establishment where the higher-ranking officers of our Intelligence services, refugees from their nearby head-quarters, can generally be found clustered thickly round the bar at opening time. There is also a sprinkling of writers.

On the same side of the street, further down among the hatters, bootmakers and purveyors of wine to the gentry and our wealthier American visitors, is Boodles, traditionally the club for gentlemen up from the country. Half-way down on the opposite side of the street stands Brooks's Club, where some faint political traditions linger from the days when Charles James Fox used regularly to lose all his money there at Faro. One of the members' more recent essays into politics was when they blackballed an ex-Cabinet Minister on the grounds that he stood in the Socialist interest.

The common factor which all three share is that the majority of their members are no longer cast in the idle, dissolute image on which their reputation for élitism was founded, but are for the most part hard-working City gents, beavering away selling insurance policies, or whatever, to each other and only asserting their claim to social exclusivity by blackballing a candidate for membership every now and again. One of their recent triumphs was to secure the exclusion of the son of an English Peer on the grounds that his grandfather had made a fortune out of selling ice-cream.

The advantage of being accepted in these charmed circles is that it still carries some atavistic prestige among the backwoodsmen and, more particularly and importantly, in the eyes of one's fellow Sherpas.

It may be of some comfort to the applicant that, in the event of his election, he will not be required to use the club to any great extent, and that to have the club's name engraved on the right-hand bottom corner of his visiting card will be enough to ensure a degree of distinction in the circles in which he hopes to move. He can then seek his amusement in less exclusive establishments or watering holes for the simply rich like Annabel's. Alternatively he may spend his time in such of those racist and élitist clubs funded by the more extreme Left Wing councils as may appeal to his particular tastes.

CHAPTER SIX

Dressing the Part

I had occasion in a previous treatise on the *mores* of the English Gentleman to tell of the reaction of one of the species when taken to task by an acquaintance who had spotted him strolling down Piccadilly in clothes which were below the highest sartorial standards.

"It doesn't matter how I dress in London," he claimed. "Nobody here knows me."

Later the same friend, visiting him in the country, again remarked upon the clothes his host was wearing.

"It doesn't matter how I dress here," he replied. "Everybody here knows me."

The point of this story is not to suggest that all gentlemen dress badly. In fact the way a gentleman dresses, particularly a country gentleman, is something that many strive to imitate – not often with conspicuous success. What is to a gentleman his workaday wardrobe never looks quite right on those who have to work hard at trying to achieve the same effect.

It is certainly true that gentlemen never *overdress*, except for rowing buffs and Scottish Lairds attending Highland balls. The generalization was that a gentleman's wardrobe contained only two suits; one for formal occasions like funerals and going up to London and the other for less formal occasions like having the vicar and his wife in for drinks. This is now less accurate than it was. Like everybody else, gentlemen have to move with the times and, as there are quite a few gentlemen who now live and work in London, wandering about in a patched tweed jacket most of the time will not do.

The Sherpa must, however, tread warily in the matter of being "well-dressed". It does *not* mean being turned out in the sort of sharp suits so beloved of pop stars and the pushier young Sloane Rangers, no matter how outrageous the prices demanded by the new crop of *avant-garde* bouffant-hair-styled tailors who have of recent years emerged from Carnaby Street and found a toe-hold in and around Savile Row and Burlington Street.

Suit Yourself

Gentlemen remain loyal to the small and exclusive group of tailors who cut suits for their fathers and their fathers' fathers. Spiralling costs have raised the price to grotesque levels, but this simply means that they take rather longer to pay. In any case, buying a suit was never regarded as a short-term investment in gentlemanly circles.

The distinctive features of a well-cut suit are that it should fit properly round the shoulders and that the buttons should be sewn on sufficiently firmly

to last at least for the lifetime of the material and
that the cuff buttons, four in number on each
sleeve, should unbutton so that they can be turned
back when washing the hands. Suits should always
be made to wear with braces and they should never
be brown.

The difference between a well-cut suit and one
"off-the-peg" can be recognized across the most
spacious drawing room and is frequently a matter
of jocular comment. As one club member
remarked about members of another club where
he had been a guest: "They seem to be quite a
decent lot of chaps. It's a pity that they all appear
to make their own trousers."

Jackets

Although, nowadays, a gentleman might well have
more than the obligatory two decent suits, it is
unlikely that they will ever reach plague proportions. Jackets are a different matter. He will have
those a-plenty and it is well known that a gentleman has never been known to throw a jacket
away. The fastidious ladies who shop for casual
clothes for the male members of their families at
those admirable Oxfam shops, if they see a half-
decent jacket, know at once that the erstwhile
owner must be dead.

Gentlemen have jackets for a catholic range of
activities – a jacket for shooting in, a fishing jacket
or a gardening jacket. Horsy gentlemen will have
a hacking jacket and golfing gentlemen a golf
jacket. Quite often they may have trousers to
match but even then they are never referred to as
a suit. By the same token a dinner jacket is never
referred to as a "dinner suit" – a dreadful solecism,

" TIGHT LINES SQUIRE! "

invented, one can only imagine, by firms who hire the things out for the benefit of those attending the annual sales conference dinner or similar functions. It would never occur to a gentleman, advised by his hostess to wear a dinner jacket, to arrive without trousers to match, nor would he turn up in a white tie only, even if expressly so instructed on the invitation.

A final word on the subject of jackets. There is no such thing in a gentleman's wardrobe as a "Sports Jacket". This phrase is generally used to describe an article of attire worn by the middle classes at weekends with flannel trousers when they want to cut a dash – rather like blazers, which come into the same category. Gentlemen hardly ever wear blazers after they leave school, where they are usually compulsory, and never the double-breasted sort with obscure crests on the pocket and polished buttons. These are regarded as the hall-mark of the cad and the bounder.

Accessories

Shirts are not garments which are generally under the control of a gentleman any more than ties are. Wives and other female relations have a habit of buying such things as birthday presents and it is obligatory that they should be greeted with cries of delight and regarded as a tribute to the taste of the female concerned. If the choice is really dis-astrous, the offending item can always be lost in the wash.

Ties present a tricky problem. To be driven, in self-defence, to wearing old school ties, regimental ties and so on is not an answer. Apart from Old Etonians and ex-rankers in the Brigade of Guards, who seem to wear their old-boy ties all the time, such ties come into the same category as blazers as the hall-mark of the socially insecure, anxious to impress all and sundry that at some time in their lives they have belonged to something or other. Old school ties should only be worn on the equivalent of Founder's Day or at weddings and Royal garden parties.

Trying to give away unwanted ties is more tricky than getting rid of shirts. I know of one man who tried to solve the problem by giving them to his gardener, which resulted not only in his nearly having a divorce on his hands but almost left him without anyone to dig the cabbage patch.

Underwear

The choice of underwear is entirely a gentleman's own affair. If he is wise he will be conventional in this respect. This means that he can please himself as to colour – so long as he chooses white. Any design will do – providing they conform to reg-ulation Army issue. Any variation from the norm might lead a wife to suspect that her husband is engaged in a clandestine love affair.

Ladies, particularly in the early stages of mar-riage, set great store by the choice of alluringly sexy flimsies designed to inspire passion in their spouses. This is something which becomes of less pressing importance with the passage of time.

One elderly dowager, on being consulted on this rather delicate matter, admitted her indifference, adding, "Personally, I always wear William's." Nowadays, this would lead to speculation as to whether they were Y-fronts or "Boxer shorts", a garment which no gentlemen will ever have heard of.

Adornments

On the matter of personal adornment, it is strongly advised that this should be kept to a minimum. In the case of professions such as bookmakers and used-car salesmen, it maybe thought to inspire confidence among clients, but otherwise it is not done to glitter like a lighthouse with such baubles as diamond tiepins, bejewelled rings, ostentatious wristwatches, flashy cuff links or gold cigarette lighters which actually work.

CHAPTER SEVEN

The Horseless Carriage

It is no longer true to say in this day and age that the natural form of locomotion for a gentleman is his horse. Indeed, for many gentlemen nowadays the horse is a positively unnatural method of doing anything, even chasing foxes or playing hockey on horseback on Smith's Lawn or Cowdray Park. But the old attitudes linger on and this is nowhere more evident than in the gentleman's attitude to his car. After all, it was not all that long ago that the horse *was* the only practical way of getting from A to B in varying forms of comfort or discomfort, and many gentlemen still regard the motor car in much the same light.

For the average gentlemen his car is not regarded as a symbol of achievement or as a projection of his *alter ego*, as it is with so many who are trying to struggle up the social scale. He tends to regard it as a somewhat regrettable necessity in this modern world, particularly as he can no longer rely on the railways for longer journeys as he did before nationalization, when, as a shareholder, they were run largely for his convenience.

That the car is now not only required, as in the old days, for such local tasks, once performed by the family gig, as popping up and down to the village, but may also be needed for quite long excursions, causes the modern gentleman to give the same care to the buying of cars as his father, or more likely his grandfather, gave to the buying of horses. That is to say it is either good at the job for which it is intended or it is a scrounger. If it shows signs of colic or the staggers or pulls up altogether, he would no more tinker with it himself than he would practise amateur surgery on his horse. He would simply damn the eyes of the villain who sold it to him, get him to put it right or find him another. He is, in fact, seldom sure, if asked, what sort of car he drives. He knows that it is a blue one and thinks it might have been made by the Japs, "or one of those foreign johnnies who are so good at it".

A gentleman who lives in the country may well have several cars – one for carrying things like bales of hay or going up and down hillsides which would test a mountain goat, and another which he uses for driving on motorways on the grounds that it uses less petrol. He may also have a car for his wife, particularly if she can afford to buy it for herself. Anything which is small and un-comfortable will do and it usually needs the brakes seeing to. A gentleman who lives in London may well not have a car at all.

" THE BUGGERS GOT STAGGERS! "

The Other Side

It implies no disrespect to those from a different
station in life, for whom the ownership of a motor
car is their greatest happiness and to own an ever
better one is their highest ambition, to demonstrate
some of the attitudes towards car-ownership which
should be avoided at all costs by the Sherpa.

There is, first of all, the Dedicated Car Owner
to whom the family car is a symbol of modest
respectability only to be used on high-days and
holidays. It is kept all week securely locked up in
its garage in company with the lawn mower,
sundry garden implements and a discarded
pushchair. It is taken out each weekend to be
washed in full view of the admiring neighbours,
most of whom will be similarly engaged. Its main
function is to take the family to the seaside on
Bank Holidays. The many hours spent entirely
stationary in the resulting traffic jams are among
the greatest rewards of family car ownership.
When taken on the annual family holiday, a sticker
proclaiming the family's destination is a top pri-
ority purchase. After some years the back window
may be completely obscured. The owners of such
cars are the salt of the earth.

It is only when we come to the upwardly
mobile that the dreadful crevasses yawn and the
ice starts to crack ominously under the Sherpa. The
yearning for some sort of social identity usually
starts with obscuring most of the front windscreen
with names like Dennis and Daphne. Sometimes
there are symbols like miniature football boots
bouncing up and down, attached to the driver's
mirror, matched by a dangling skeleton or a witch
on a broomstick or some slogan on the rear

window like "Water-skiers do it standing up" or "My other car is a BMW". These are supposed to entertain those who have just been pushed past with a fine flourish and much hooting of horns.

From this it is but a small step to rather grander and faster cars, many of which are fitted with hooks above the side windows on which to hang jackets or blazers. These are driven at great speed, with much flashing of lights, cutting in on the inside lane and two-fingered jabbings in the air, mostly by toothpaste salesmen desperate to sell another tube or two before the shops shut. Their "Get out of my way, you peasant!" attitude aspires to Aristocracy, but they are social mountaineers who have badly lost their way. Once the Sherpa has gone thus far astray there is little hope that he will ever get back on to the right track.

The next stage can only be the purchase of something like a Rolls Royce with smoked glass windows and one of those thingummys on the radiator in gold, together with a Range Rover, with a leaping fish or a retriever with a pheasant in its mouth screwed on to the bonnet, which hopelessly misguided mountaineers use for shopping in Haslemere High Street.

Again, once that stage has been reached there is little hope of them getting out of the crevasse into which they have fallen.

CHAPTER EIGHT

The Gentleman's House

The student who has studied the trap into which the car-buying Sherpa can fall by being led on to thinner and thinner ice until it cracks under the weight of his ostentation will, I hope, accept some friendly advice when it comes to considering the all-important matter of his house.

By tradition gentlemen live in very large houses which they have inherited, together with such trappings once considered essential to his life style as family portraits, stuffed trophies of the chase, crumbling furniture and large built-in bookcases with glass doors, to which the keys have long since been lost. These are full of leather-bound books, many of them volumes of sermons.

The gentleman's house will also have certain rooms not usually to be found in less imaginatively designed homes: a gunroom, a servants' hall, a butler's pantry, laundry rooms, game larders and a housekeeper's room. Such houses are also extremely cold and the indoor sanitation is rather primitive.

It is not suggested that the aspiring Sherpa

should attempt to live under such conditions and indeed many gentlemen have themselves given up the struggle and moved to much more modest residences like the stables or the old gamekeeper's or gardener's cottage.

However, especially in the country, it is only persons of unquestionable social status who can afford to live in really reduced circumstances.

At the same time it is only pop stars and Arab sheiks who can get away with the vulgarity of buying large mansions and installing gold bath taps and swimming pools, without which gentlemen have managed for so many generations.

For the Sherpa to attempt the same thing would quite destroy his prospects in the world to which he hopes to belong. He is, therefore, faced with a considerable dilemma. He cannot move into some workman's cottage lest it be thought that it represents his true place in society. He cannot set himself up in marbled halls with a fleet of Rolls Royces, blazers, dark glasses and servants, and expect to be taken for anything other than a pop star or a barrow boy made good.

The answer is that he should find himself a place in the country – by country I mean anywhere outside Surrey, Buckinghamshire and most of Sussex – which constitutes outer suburbia nowadays. Old Rectories are all right, so are mills and abandoned farmhouses but *not* oast houses. There he can surround himself and his family with the sort of trappings which might be expected of a gentleman.

These do not include fitted cocktail bars, vast television sets, elaborate Hi-Fi systems, cigarette boxes which play "I'm dreaming of a White

" EVER THOUGHT OF PUTTING IN TROUT ? "

Christmas" or any of those admittedly ingenious pieces of furniture which, at the press of a button, turn into something else – like settees which become Put-U-Ups or beds which disappear into cupboards.

On the subject of bathrooms, there is certainly no obligation to try and reproduce the sort of sanitary arrangements which tend to be traditional in gentlemen's houses, with huge, brown-stained bathtubs with dripping taps or water-closets enclosed in mahogany boxes. Beware of bathroom "suites" in "tasteful" colours like crushed black-currant or liquidized avocado, however. You can also safely ignore the creeping Continental fashion of installing things like bidets unless you feel they might be useful for the children to sail their boats in.

Country Style

There is little point in the Sherpa acquiring a house in the country, however strategically placed, if he is not prepared to assume at least the veneer of a country gentleman. This means that his house should suggest a long-standing pre-occupation with such rustic pursuits as hunting, shooting and fishing and demonstrate a careless disregard for the precise mathematics so beloved by the professional interior decorator. Of all rooms in the country house the hall is by far the most important in establishing the general atmosphere. By and large, all that is needed is a plethora of such things as raincoats, gumboots, tennis racquets and walking sticks of all shapes and sizes, with plenty of sporting or military prints on the walls and overflowing into the downstairs wash-and-brush-up accommodation, which should be at least large enough to serve as a gunroom as well. Having got that right you will be more than half the way there.

Town Style

If the location and style of a gentleman's country house is important, the same applies to his London residence. There are, indeed, few, if any, of the *ancien régime* who have managed to retain their London houses from the days of their former glory. In this respect, both the upper classes and the arrivistes are on the same footing.

Until the outbreak of the last war it was considered impossible to live outside the boundaries of Mayfair or Belgravia, though a certain tolerance was shown to a few eccentrics who elected to live in the better parts of Chelsea and restricted areas in Kensington.

All that has changed. To have a house, or, worse, a flat, however large and grand, in W.1 or S.W.1 does not carry any social status at all. The available accommodation has been snapped up by multi-national corporations, Arab oil sheiks, ladies of easy virtue and gambling racketeers the origins of whose wealth is not always easy to establish. This particularly applies to black spots like the once prestigious Eaton Square, now converted into a veritable rabbit-warren. A far more acceptable alternative is a modest, formerly working-class house in a place like the World's End, the wrong end of the Fulham Road or even Battersea. In no circumstances should the latter be described as South Chelsea.

Oddly enough, places like Maida Vale have never really lived down their reputation for being only suitable for gentleman's mistresses (now an almost extinct breed) or Hampstead as a breeding ground for woolly middle-class intellectuals.

Other once outside-the-pale locations for gentlemanly residences which are coming up on the rails are Clapham, pronounced Cla'aam (overlooking the Common), Brixton (not overlooking the prison) and Kennington, where there is a good chance of having the Prince of Wales as your landlord. The belief that the Duchy of Cornwall is far too gentlemanly to sue for such trifles as non-payment of rent is, alas, untrue.

CHAPTER NINE

Beware of the Dog

Of all the objects, animate or inanimate, with which the Sherpa should equip himself as his aids in his arduous struggle to the upper peaks, none are of greater importance than his dogs. Here is a quotation from *The Observer* from as long ago as 13 April, 1806, which will serve to confirm the truth of this observation.

Headed *Singular Conviction*, it read:

A Curate of a village near a town and one of the Overseers of the Parish, a gentleman farmer, had a dispute respecting some private business, and the Farmer d——d the Clergyman's eyes. For this offence he was brought before the Magistrates at Marlborough Street, and convicted in the penalty of 5s. The Farmer contended that he was not a gentleman, and that he ought not to pay more than 1s. This was overruled on the grounds that *he kept his sporting dogs* [my italics] and took his wine after dinner.

Quite recently a Ms Francesca Findlater wrote yet another of the many books devoted to guiding the footsteps of the social climber, but this one was devoted entirely to the subject of which dogs were U and which non-U – in other words which dogs were good for the gentlemanly image and which were not. To quote Ms Findlater:

> Having the right dog is just as important to the social aspirer and those already at the top of the social ladder as going to the right school and not planting Hybrid Tea Roses in your garden.

Ho-hum. I do not know whether the planting of Hybrid Tea Roses in your garden constitutes a social gaffe because I have no idea what a Hybrid Tea Rose looks like. I have already given my views about going to the "right" school, but I whole-heartedly agree with the bit about the importance of having the "right" dog. I am not so sure that I agree what constitutes a "right" dog as opposed to a "wrong" dog. Ms Findlater describes "a top person's dog" as a "Sloane Rover". This does not inspire confidence.

Any suggestion that the monstrous regiment of Sloane Rangers are "top people" must surely be laid to rest if, as the book insists, they "make their puppies especially welcome with cat-shaped hot-water bottles" and give birthday parties where the dog guests drink champagne and have their own birthday cake. When the book goes on to claim that some dogs actually own £1,500 silver hand-engraved bowls and monogrammed cashmere blankets at £600 a throw, one begins to think that the authoress must be joking, but she is not.

The Gentleman's Dog

The truth is that very few gentlemen keep a dog in London, though their wives and children may do so.

Anything quite small and not yappy will do, and
the gentleman may even come to regard it with
affection, particularly if it is a Jack Russell ter-
rier. Some of the better class families go so far
as to have two, three, or even more, and happily
put up with their persecution of most things that
move, from cats to young children. This is an
indulgence not extended to many of the smaller
breeds like those packs of Corgis which surround
the Queen's person.

The sort of dog a gentleman owns is one of
the sporting breeds, with labradors at the top of
the list and retrievers, pointers and spaniels of
various sorts also high in the popularity stakes.
They are for the most part working dogs which
are kept in kennels. When they get old they are
allowed into the house, after which they are apt
to become very fat, occupy the best chairs and
smell horribly.

Ms Findlater finally goes completely off the rails
and advises that, if you wish to give the impression
that you are landed gentry, get a huge dog like a
Dobermann which is "excellent for protecting the
family heirlooms".

If there are any dogs to which no gentleman
would ever give house room they are those wal-
loping great things like Dobermanns, Great Danes
and Alsatians, and to hell with protecting the
family heirlooms. Such dogs are invariably owned
by small, rather insignificant people who keep them
to tow their owners down to the pubs in outer
suburbia of a Sunday morning in an effort to attract
attention. In this they are often successful, even if the
only effect is for the other customers to move to the
further end of the bar.

"PUT IT DOWN BUTCHER!"

CHAPTER TEN

On Being a Sport

In no sphere of activity is it more difficult for the Sherpa to find recognition than in the sporting field, and yet it is there that it is of the utmost importance to find acceptance.

Traditionally the most prestigious sports are the most expensive, and are yearly becoming more so. Grouse shooting, salmon fishing and, to a much more limited extent nowadays, fox hunting, are all passports to social acceptance.

Fox hunting is not now regarded by many as a field sport at all, but rather as an elaborate way of taking exercise, like the dreadful middle-class craze for jogging. It is also generally recognized that what competitors in Miss World beauty competitions insist on describing as their favourite hobby of "horse-back riding" has distinct sexual connotations, *après-hunt* carryings-on are at least as important as *après-ski* activities after a day on the slippery slopes. "Sex maniacs, the lot of them," an old farmer was heard to comment recently as he watched the field gallop across his winter wheat.

This tends to demote hunting to the second eleven, along with such sporting activities as chalet ski-ing parties, surf boarding, skin-diving and continuing to play rugger after the age of twenty-five.

Still clinging to first-tcam status in the equine world is three-day eventing and, among ball games, real tennis. Tennis of the vicarage lawn variety is acceptable, but not if it is played at a tennis club. It is also quite all right to tour with your own cricket side up to the age of sixty-five, after which you should have your head examined.

Games like snooker, billiards, bowls and croquet have always been top people's sports, but they are now seriously endangered by the encroaching tide of professionalism.

Racquets remains socially preferable to squash which has taken on the connotations of those dreaded "sports complexes" which are springing up all over the place. Golf should only be played in Scotland.

Of all sporting activities, however, there are none in which the Sherpa is more likely to come a cropper than shooting and fishing.

The first trap is that, although any form of blood-sport is an extremely expensive business, any form of ostentation or display of wealth is the surest way of slipping to the bottom of the social scale and becoming a figure of fun. It is as well to remember a guide-line laid down by R. S. Surtees as to who was or was not a gentleman. He declared: "The only infallible rule we know, is that the man who is always talking about being a gentleman never is one."

The fellow who goes round with fishing flies stuck in his hat, or sporting mascots on the bonnet of his motor car, for that matter, is a good example. The only time a gentleman might have a fishing fly stuck in his hat by mistake is on the river bank. It is also unwise to mention: "the pair of Purdeys which I always keep in the boot of my Rolls". This does not go down well with impoverished gentlemen who can scarcely afford the price of cartridges and have to let their shooting.

The real crunch for the Sherpa comes when he actually has to appear armed on the field of battle. Strolling down Sloane Street in a pair of green wellies with little straps at the top or along Piccadilly in a Barbour jacket and a felt hat is all very well but it will not cut much ice when you are in your grouse butt or standing at your peg in a pheasant drive waiting for the action to begin.

It is not so tricky for the ostentatiously horsey set. Most people at point-to-points can cut a decent figure surrounded by picnic baskets, shooting sticks and tweedy young ladies in headscarves and *"Je Reviens"*. The nearest they need come to the action is the other end of a decent pair of field glasses. Even those who get on to a horse at the start of a day's hunting while the stirrup cup is being passed round can just about pass muster, providing they can remember which side to get aboard.

Shooting

It is not necessary, when out shooting, to dress up like a Christmas tree, festooned with dog whistles, cartridge extractors or ammunition belts. In fact, to do so will make them thoroughly suspect especially – and most importantly – by the keepers and beaters.

Now that syndicate shoots have become the order of the day the performance of "the guns" making their first appearance is unknown, but the experienced head keeper has long since learned to read the signs. In the old days he would call his army together before the first drive and mark their cards for them: "Afraid we have Major Blethering-Bootstrap with us today, so watch it. He has drawn Number Three in the first drive. Lord Poore-Shotte is at number one so keep your heads down on the right flank."

Nowadays, with no known form to go by, the briefing of the beaters is more likely to go something like this: "We've got a couple of right 'uns in the middle. Baseball hats, yellow jackets, the lot. And there is a dangerous-looking cove at the far end, strutting around like a turkey cock and bellowing like a bull, fit to frighten all the dogs."

Of course, appearances can be deceptive. Foreigners are apt to turn themselves out rather oddly, particularly Americans, who insist on wrapping themselves in so much brightly-coloured protective clothing that they look like walking advertisements for Michelin tyres. Nevertheless some of them are very good shots. The trouble is that the beaters are apt to go to ground when they find themselves opposite a dubious-looking "gun", which, good and safe shot though he may be, rather spoils his chances of getting much shooting.

Above all, the main thing is to remember what one is supposed to be shooting at. Not everything that moves is to be regarded as fair game. The main things that you should not shoot, in order of importance, are: one's host, one's host's dog, dogs belonging to fellow guests and one's fellow guests.

" OH, AND A WHITE FLAG MEANS THE BEATERS HAVE SURRENDERED! "

Keepers and beaters come further down the list, but remember that they have ways of getting their own back.

At the Waterside

Just as it is a wise man who treats the head keeper with the greatest respect when out shooting, so will a wise man treat his ghillie on the river – only more so. A mixture of awe and reverence is required.

It would be the height of folly, for example, not to ask his advice on the state of the water, even though you can see that perfectly well for yourself, or to fail to consult him on what fly to use. It is also tactful to establish at an early stage how he likes his whisky.

Generally speaking, there is no one a ghillie warms to more readily than the chap who confesses his ignorance, unlike the gamekeeper, who prefers those who at least know the rough direction in which to point the gun.

I can remember fishing alongside an American gentleman whose complete ignorance of anything to do with the art of casting a fly was threatening to try the patience of even the most saintly of ghillies. Every few casts his line would finish up in a bird's nest of a muddle at intervals between becoming attached to everything from the nearest bush to the bottom of the river. It seemed that the ghillie had finally run out of patience and had turned his back to walk away, when the American let out an agonized cry. There was a tremendous splash – a large salmon had somehow become attached to his fly. Alas, before the ghillie could reach his side the line broke. The American reeled in his slack line ruefully. "Well I'll be danged," he marvelled. "Do you know, that goddam fish has just chewed the bug off the end of my bit of string." It quite made everybody's day. The ghillie was later heard to refer to him as "a proper gent".

By contrast, another ghillie had the misfortune of rowing a fisherman to and fro all day long in the pouring rain without any result, while the know-all fisherman warmed himself against the bitter cold with constant draughts from his large whisky flask without having the courtesy to offer a dram to the ghillie. Finally, to add to his discontent, his matchbox got so wet that he could not light his cigar. "Is there nowhere in this damned boat dry enough to strike a match?" he complained. "You could try the back of my throat," remarked his thoroughly browned-off attendant.

In this case it was the ghillie who proved himself to be the gentleman. Remember that a gentleman is never unintentionally rude.

Other Sports

There was a time when to go abroad for winter sports usually meant that the ground was too hard for hunting at home. It was in fact the English hunting set who "invented" ski-ing. They also invented tobogganing, or rather exported it to Switzerland, as well as making skating and curling fashionable. Today tobogganing (particularly down the Cresta Run at St Moritz, another British upper-crust invention) and skating remain very much upper class. Ski-ing is less so now that the once-exclusive slopes are crowded with vast numbers of people who can enjoy a packaged fortnight in the second best hotels for much the same price as an out-of-season week in Blackpool.

One way or another ski-ing trips nowadays do not do much for the social image, just as packaged holidays anywhere in Europe have become decidedly downmarket. Only Russia, India and the Himalayas are really safe.

All of which comes back to the question of money which we have already discussed. It might be tempting to conclude that the greater the amount of money spent on a holiday the higher it should rate in the social climber's handbook. A chips-with-everything blow-out in Benidorm should be somewhere near the bottom of the list and those fabulously expensive faraway "paradise islands" at the top end. However, it does not work that way. Most established gentry would regard swanning off to somewhere like Mustique as inexpressibly vulgar. Anyway it is hard to get a booking to such places nowadays because Television Companies bag all the best seats for the winners of their parlour games.

Doing Something

What it really boils down to is that traditionally gentlemen never took holidays. They went to places to *do things*, even if it meant travelling abroad: big game hunting, following bull fights, amateur botanical or zoological expeditions, for instance. Today, with the need for so many gentlemen to engage in gainful employment, with the resulting restrictions on the amount of time they can devote to their traditional sports and pastimes, very few would consider spending good money just to go and sit in the sun, or to jostle with the hordes of people with whom they have, perforce, to spend much of their daily lives and from whom they seek escape.

Paradoxes

The mystique of successful participation in gentlemanly sports in general, and huntin', shootin' and fishin' in particular, must appear from the foregoing to rely on a series of contradictions.

That the shooting man, for example, should find it perfectly logical to include a generous subscription to the Royal Society for the Protection of Birds in totting up the annual cost of cartridges and other engines of destruction would seem to many not to be logical. On the contrary, it is extremely logical, for how could he enjoy his sport if there were no birds for him to destroy?

That he should despise ostentation while prizing the most ostentatiously expensive sports above all others, is just another of those equations which, if the Sherpa can solve it satisfactorily, will put him that much nearer the top of the mountain.

CHAPTER ELEVEN

Guidelines

Before we go on to a final analysis of what is considered U and non-U in this changing world it might be useful to list one or two traps to avoid, as well as giving aspiring gentlemen a few hints on how to recognize a real one if he meets one.

Personal Accessories

There are one or two small details in the way in which a gentleman dresses which are useful to note. When I brought out an earlier work, I was much taken to task over a mild observation that it is customary for a gentleman to wear his handkerchief up his sleeve, or tucked into his cuff. The book gave rise to a lengthy correspondence in such august newspapers as *The Daily Telegraph* and *The Times*. The final nail in the coffin of the "one-for-show-and-one-for-blow" brigade, who advocated carrying one handkerchief in the trouser pocket and another, purely for show, in the breast pocket of the jacket, was adroitly driven home by a distinguished Bishop. He posed the interesting question

"HE SIMPLY WILL NOT GET HIS TAILOR TO MAKE HIM A SUIT FOR COLDS!"

as to whether, when overcome with emotion during a funeral oration, his congregation would prefer that he dabbed his eyes with a handkerchief from his sleeve or that he hitched up his surplice and rummaged about for one in the hem of his ecclesiastical knickers.

Not only the clergy, but gentlemen wearing uniform have for generations carried their handkerchiefs up their sleeves. It is a practice that aspiring gentlemen would be well advised to adopt, suggesting as it does a respect for ancestral tradition.

Warning has already been given about the wearing of gaudy accessories in the way of personal jewellery in the hope of impressing others with evidence of wealth. This does not altogether preclude the wearing of cufflinks, although gold, and preferably crested, links should only be worn with evening dress, and possibly gold studs, bearing in mind, of course, that these should be worn with an evening shirt and under no circumstances in the ears. Gentlemen never wear diamonds but a pearl tiepin might be just passable on such occasions as Ladies' Day at Ascot.

Creditability

Although gentlemen are not given to carrying large amounts of money on their persons, still less are they given to loading their notecases with credit cards. The ultimate in vulgarity are those who keep every conceivable variety of credit card in a specially constructed kind of plastic holder which they take every opportunity of displaying.

The point is that no gentleman would dream of playing host at any establishment where they would not accept his personal cheque without demur. His cheque book would be unlikely to advertise any of the Big Five high street banks, unless he happened to have become a Director of one of them. Nor would a gentleman buy an article in a shop where they would not put it on his account. The need for a plastic guarantee of his solvency never arises, therefore.

More about that cheque book. Gentlemen never have joint accounts with their wives. Even if she is frightfully rich and he is frightfully poor it is something that simply is not done.

Household Hints

In London, where once it was never done to live in a house which had a street number, only in one with a name, like Londonderry House, Crewe House or Grosvenor House, now it is only done to live in a house which *has* a number and never a name, especially not The Chestnuts or Acacia Villa.

In the country it is necessary to live in a house which has a name, even if it is in the village high street. The country house should preferably be defined as a Manor, Grange, Lodge, even Rectory or Mill, or, in extreme cases, Castle.

It is very bad form to have one of those unsightly and deliberately conspicuous burglar alarm boxes stuck on the wall of your London house, advertising to any potential burglar the system on which your alarm is supposed to work and to your friends that you have possessions of immense value to protect. In most cases your friends are more gullible than the burglars, which perhaps justifies the expense in terms of upward social mobility.

Travel Tips

The easiest and surest way of identifying a gentleman when travelling is by his luggage. A gentleman never has smart luggage which looks expensive. Least of all would he have luggage with someone else's initials stamped all over it. This extraordinary habit springs from the urge, apparently, to impress on all and sundry that the luggage is even more expensive than it looks. Research shows that the repetitive use of LV indicates that it is made by Louis Vuitton, apparently the top luggage-making firm, and a P indicates that it comes from a French dress-maker called Pierre Cardin. I am also given to understand that a large and ornate L indicates that it comes from the Earl of Lichfield, although I very much doubt if the chap makes the luggage himself.

A gentleman's luggage will be made of heavy leather, with labels stuck all over it: P & O or Bombay and instructions like "Not Wanted on Voyage" or "Cabin 504". Of course a lot of gentle-men have come to realize, in these days of air travel, that such relics from the family attic are too heavy to be practical, so they invest in some-thing lighter, but if it has anyone's name or initials stamped on it it will be their own.

Gentlemen almost always travel first class on the railway from force of habit, but never on an aeroplane. This is partly because they cannot afford it and partly for fear of being trampled underfoot by pop stars or businessmen hurrying off some-where to sell something.

"RIGHT INITIALS WRONG LOGO — DUMMY!"

Shopping Hints

The gentleman's aversion to carrying advertising on his luggage extends to his wife when it comes to shopping in top people's stores like Harrod's, whose carrier bags are so treasured by the masses. This springs only partly from a disinclination to advertise the name of their grocer, but largely from the admittedly old-fashioned idea that groceries were something that were delivered in a van and not something that a lady ought to have to go out and haggle over in the market place then drag home in a bag.

A Personal Matter

Fashions change, as I have been at pains to point out, but perhaps no change has been more dramatic than in the matter of the various forms of facial adornment of the English male.

There was a time when it was almost *de rigueur* for Army Officers to grow a closely clipped and disciplined moustache which tended to get larger and bushier with promotion to a more senior rank. In Victorian and Edwardian days beards were all the go, particularly among the more *nouveau riche* of Edward VII's cronies and among social climbers in respectable business circles. The practice became less prevalent during the reign of the bearded King George V and was restricted largely to Naval Officers, Arctic explorers and a few eccentric artists. It practically died out during the reigns of two bare-chinned kings and one queen.

The revival of the beard is of comparatively recent origin, having been adopted largely by whizz kids in the advertising business and others suffering from emotional and social insecurity. Few of them survive after the age of thirty, with some notable exceptions like Prince Michael of Kent.

Moustaches are a different matter. Practically overnight they have become the recognition signal for adults eager to indulge in homosexual practices. The result has been queues of young officers outside Boots the Chemists in Aldershot clamouring for shaving cream and razor blades.

CHAPTER TWELVE

U and non-U Updated

This final chapter is largely devoted to the subject of U and non-U speech which, since the publication of *Noblesse Oblige*, has been the object of such intense heart-searching among those who seek to advance socially and on which so much rubbish has since been published in various "authoritative" guides.

There are certain words and turns of phrase which are apt to set upper-class teeth on edge. (Not, let it be noted, "dentures", as good an example as any of the sort of genteelism which is apt to let the side down.) It is, however, very often the context in which a word is used, rather than the word itself, which betrays those modest origins which the Sherpa is so anxious to conceal.

Rather than make a definitive list on a subject which is not definable, I have chosen to place the infelicitous words and phrases into groups and situations in which they are most likely to occur.

By using this method it is inevitable that the short essays which follow should be as much concerned with U and non-U behaviour as with words. I make no excuse for this, because the term has now been given far wider application than the mere use and misuse of words. U and non-U is an expression which has come to embrace a whole life style.

Eating Your Words

There is no time when the Sherpa should be more mindful of his p's and q's than when eating out. As this is not a book on social etiquette, I shall not bother the reader with such matters as how to handle a knife and fork, in which direction to circulate the port, or even such invaluable advice as to how to achieve more than one's fair share of the stuff in the process.

Eating out nowadays is not what it used to be. Gentlemen, as a class, were never great eaters-out in public places, preferring their clubs or their homes. If they did eat out it was usually in the great and respected hotels in London: the Ritz or the old Berkeley Hotel across the road. In the provinces, gentlemen chose the then excellent Station Hotels which were run entirely for their convenience until the nationalization of the railways and the advent of more liberal expense accounts for commercial travellers.

Today, what with the shortage of domestic staff and little places with foreign-sounding names springing up at every corner, we have become a nation of eaters-out and it is not surprising that styles should have changed – the most noticeable change being the general lack of any style at all.

A good example is the quite appalling habit which has spread like a prairie fire, fuelled by a great new army of writers who have arbitrarily assumed the role of "experts" on the subject of wine and food, of referring to the first course as "Starters".

The picture which this conjures up of rows of eaters, knives and forks at the ready, waiting for the pistol so that they can race each other over six courses to the finishing line, is not an attractive one. "Starters" is a very non-U word indeed.

By the same token, the word "Afters" should not be used for the pudding course. It is much on a par with "Sweets", suggesting, as it does, a few bulls'-eyes or a packet of Smarties.

It is largely the restaurants and the food "critics" who are to blame for vulgarizing the vocabulary once laid down by the more elegant establishments. It seems to me that they thoroughly deserve each other.

The sort of writer who burbles on about "sampling" the whatsit, "while my partner elected for the something else" is enough to put one off anything he or she (for there are lots of women at the game) may see fit to recommend. More importantly from the point of view of the social climber, phrases like: "I think I'll sample the [or worse still 'your'] roast beef", instead of simply, "I'm going to have roast beef", is an example of the unhappy choice of phrase which is the hallmark of the chap who is trying too hard. It is this sort of false pretension which is such a giveaway and applies in even greater measure when it comes to the question of wine.

Winemanship

There is a prevalent belief that a gentleman knows everything about wine, or even that to know all about wine is to be a gentleman.

It is not simply a matter, as Jorrocks put it, that "Champagne certainly gives one werry gentlemanly ideas". It springs from the concept that a gentleman is someone who takes wine with his meal. *Ipso facto*, to demonstrate that one knows all about wines is proof positive that one was brought up as a gentleman.

The traps into which the Sherpa who subscribes to this belief may fall are legion. He is an easily-detected species from the moment the wine waiter pours the first few drops into his glass for him to taste. When he starts sniffing and sipping and peering at it against the light, as if debating whether to order a hundred cases or more, the wine snob gives himself away. He is only being asked, after all, to confirm that the wine he has ordered with so much huffing and puffing is not "corked" and can be drunk safely. A quick sniff is enough to establish that.

If the wine which he has ordered should, on tasting, not come up to his exacting standards, he feels entitled to send it back; this will have the waiters doubling up with mirth and happily replacing it with an inferior wine at twice the price. A prize example of wine snobbery was the man who sent back his *coq au vin* on the grounds that he suspected that the *vin* in which the *coq* had been cooked was non-vintage.

Then, of course, there are the dogmas about wine learned by rote by the socially insecure. "Red wine with meat, white wine with fish," they chant like a litany. Rubbish, of course. Why one should not have a decent claret with Dover sole has never been clear to me – or any other claret lover.

Red wine must be served at "room temperature", whatever that may be. White wine must be chilled . . . All rubbish, but dear to the heart of he who takes such pains to demonstrate that he knows "what's what". In the opinion of most reasonable people, anyone who allows the champagne to remain in its ice bucket for longer than ten minutes or so is inviting a sharp attack of the Bombay Trots.

Table Manners

It is natural enough that he who seeks to impress with his *savoir faire* should take the opportunities offered by a candle-lit dinner to prove it. This generally takes the form of complaining about everything. After all why should he put up with a *Tournedos Chasseur* not up to the low standards of the Nursery, even if Nanny did teach him to pronounce it "Tornado Chaser"?

Gentlemen eating out very seldom complain or send anything back. They simply make a mental note not to eat there again. The finger-snapper with a compulsion to send for the head waiter to complain about everything from the temperature of the Montrachet to the flavour of the sorbet should, at least, try to avoid that dreadful vulgarism: calling for the Maitre D. Presumably it is some sort of shorthand for the French *Maitre d'Hotel*, but in England he is known as the Head Waiter.

A wise man treats the Head Waiter, whom he usually knows by name, as a friend. To gain his respect and that of the Head Doorman, in some ways an even more important functionary, and to be regarded as a "perfect gentleman" by them is an important step up the social ladder. You will get much better service and never want for a taxi, even in a thunderstorm.

Fieldcraft

The greatest single trap when talking about things that are hunted, shot or fished for is to refer to them in the plural when they should be referred to in the singular or *vice versa*. To get this wrong is the most dreadful give-away.

To illustrate this curiosity of linguistics at its most simple, let us take fox hunting. You can quite properly go fox-hunting or hunt foxes but you cannot hunt fox. There is nothing particularly difficult about that, but game birds are more complicated.

You can go pheasant shooting or partridge shooting and shoot pheasants and partridges but for some reason there are a great number of people, who would not dream of "hunting fox", who will talk about shooting pheasant or partridge, which is very non-U indeed. Life is not made easier, particularly for Americans, by the fact that most game birds, singly or in quantities, have no plural at all. It is correct to go shooting (or "hunting", as Americans will insist on calling it) birds such as woodcock, snipe and all species of duck. Goose is the exception. You only shoot geese.

While on the subject of the correct use of the singular and plural, it is very non-U to have a billiard room in your house, even if you have room for one, which quite a few people do not

" NOT TOO COLD ONCE YOU'RE IN SIR! "

nowadays. The game is called billiards, not billiard,
and it is played in a billiards room on a billiards
table, on which you can also play a game called
snookers. A gentleman will still challenge another
gentleman to a game of snookers. It is a habit
Sherpas would be wise to adopt, if only to demonstrate that they have been properly brought
up. In the same way, while a hunting coat is
correctly described as "pink", it is, in fact, bright
red. Fellow Sherpas will take you for an ignorant
fellow if you show awareness of this anomaly.
Anyone who needs reminding that fox hounds are
not dogs will never make it as a Sherpa.

To return to the shooting and fishing scene,
while it is quite in order to ask, "What was the
bag?" after a day's shooting, you do not talk about
"bagging a couple of pheasants", unless, of course,
you have actually stolen them, any more than it is
done to talk about "grassing" a fish when you
mean landed it. The term "grassing" is, however,
quite correct when used to describe killing a stag.
All very difficult and confusing.

Being Tidy about the House

As this essay on U and non-U words seems to be
developing into a grammar lesson, it might be
helpful to describe certain words in common use
about the house as being passively U as opposed to
those which are actively non-U.

Words in the passively U category often concern such new-fangled devices as refrigerators or
vacuum cleaners. While there is nothing non-U
about calling a refrigerator a refrigerator, or even,
one must reluctantly concede, a "fridge", most of
the old school tend to stick to the old brand names

and refer to a refrigerator as a "Frigidaire", in the
same way that they would call a sewing machine a
"Singer" and a vacuum cleaner a "Hoover". In
fact, Hoover must now be regarded as part of the
English language. Who, even today, would talk
about "vacuum-cleaning" a room! Although it has
become a charming anachronism, an elderly
gentleman of my acquaintance refers to crossing
the Atlantic on the *Queen Elizabeth* as going by
"steamer". On the other hand most gentlemen
who have radios still turn on the wireless to listen
to the news.

Actively non-U

While it is not actively non-U to call a wireless set
a radio, particularly if it is in a motor car, it is
actively non-U to refer to the television set as the
"telly". TV is possible – but only just. Abbrevia-
tions are, on the whole, dangerous and should be
avoided.

Of all domestic issues, however, there is none
where controversy rages more furiously than when
it comes to indoor sanitation. I think it was Nancy
Mitford who first laid down that the upper classes
always called a lavatory a lavatory. That is, and
always has been, partly true. Not to be shy about
calling a spade a spade is something which the
upper and working classes have always had in
common. It is only the various grades of the
middle classes who go into paroxysms about it.
Such genteel circumlocutions as "It" or "The
Littlest Room", or that strange Americanism "The
John", which are used by middle-class matrons in
their semi-detached homes, are only slightly
removed from such Sloane-Ranger-approved

words as "The Loo", possibly derived from the French *Lieu*, meaning "The Place", a coy euphemism once used by the bourgeoisie too prim to use the more robust word "Toilette". Today, in its anglicized form "toilet", it is a word which the social-climbing middle classes shy away from as being the epitome of suburbanism and a matter for condign punishment should their children, who "pick up these dirty words at school, my dear", ever use it.

Which all goes to show what a lot of rubbish it all is. In fact, nothing is more give-away than the self-conscious use of what have come to be considered "right" or U words.

It was, perhaps, unfortunate that long after the Mitford joke had run its course, the publishing house of Debrett took upon itself the task, in a book called *U and Non-U Revisited*, not only to perpetuate, in all seriousness, some of the more light-hearted Mitfordisms, like declaring mantelpiece, mirror, notepaper and hand bag to be lower-class words, but to invent a whole new crop of apparently non-U words. Thus, according to the Editor, Mr Buckle, and "his brilliant friends" (*sic*), only the lower classes have cereal for breakfast, wear corsets, have dandruff, sit in a lounge, eat pastries, wear a raincoat, refer to a woman as a lady or the Royal Family generically as the Royals, or call anything which comes from Scotland Scottish.

The upper classes, declared this brilliant coterie of friends, only ever have "cornflakes, etc." for breakfast, wear stays, have scurf, never sit in anything but a drawing-room (even in a ship or an hotel), only eat cake and only wear a raincoat if a mackintosh is not available. No female should ever be referred to as anything other than a woman. To talk about the Royals is unforgiveably lower class; they should be referred to as "Royalties"; while all things Scottish should be referred to as Scotch. This runs counter to the long-held belief that all things from north of the Border are Scottish, with the exception of whisky, thistles, mist and butterscotch.

Thus the non-U person, overcome by nausea in an hotel lounge, would quite destroy any pretensions to being a person of social standing were he to demand of a lady the way to the toilet as he was going to be sick. The upper-class person, caught in a similar predicament in an hotel drawing-room, would command a woman to show him to the lavatory, where he wished to be ill.

The Sloane Ranger, by contrast, according to a later manual for the guidance of the middle classes, would simply vomit or, more correctly, apparently, in Sloane Ranger parlance, "shoot the cat" in his, or, preferably, someone else's hat.

Whilst, generally speaking, euphemisms of any sort are to be avoided as smacking of the middle classes, perhaps it is really better that the Sherpa should ignore this dictum and do or say, as the upper classes have always done, just what they damn well please.

Most "polite" euphemisms among the upper classes have their origins in Nanny's teaching in the nursery. Their charges either abandon these in later life or continue to use them to the end of their days.

Who could, for example, fault a no-nonsense, high-born lady who not only persisted throughout her life in calling one of the more unmentionable parts of her body a "botty" but customarily referred to breaking wind as a "botty cough"?

Better that if you can, you elegant ladies from Penge.

By comparison to shy off calling the toilet "The Toilet" is really dreadfully self-conscious middle class.

Envoi

In asserting that by following the rules, and avoiding the more obvious crevasses, it is possible, in our new upwardly mobile society, to become accepted as a gentleman in one's own life time, it is also wise to remember that you are in a highly competitive business and that it is the most newly-elected to the ranks of the élite who will be the most jealous of their new-found exclusivity.

Quite frankly the Old Brigade have long since handed over the baton and don't give a damn. None of them go chuntering on about the vulgarity of having fish knives, milk in first or anything like that any more. You will even find some of impeccable lineage who have deliberately adopted working-class phrases and call their machines "the Telly" and refer to their parents as "Our Mum and Dad" . . .

So beware! When you feel that you have joined the chosen few at the top of the social pile, it would

be a mistake to relax too comfortably in your leather armchair.

There will be plenty of your fellow *nouveaux arrivistes* at the summit of the icy peak who will be only too delighted to find an opportunity to stick an icicle up your arse.

Dictionary note:

Arse. (U.S. ass): (now vulg) n. the buttocks – n, arse'hole (U.S. ass'hole), the anus (vulg).

Oh dearie, dearie me. I wonder what the Russian is for all that.